# ★★★ Football's ★★★
# MOST CONTROVERSIAL
# CALLS

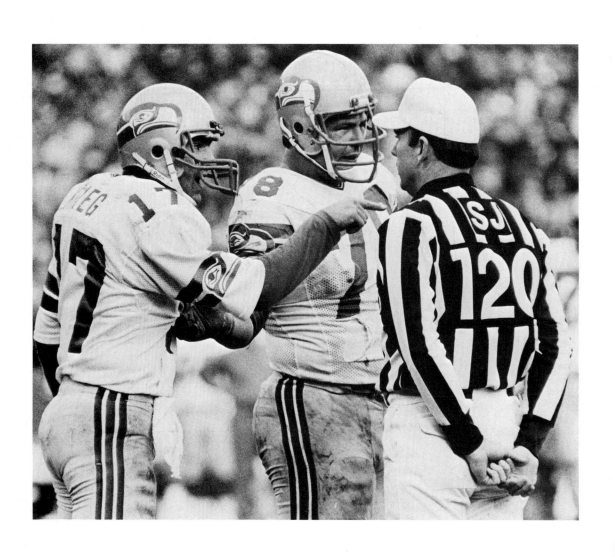

# ★★★ Football's ★★★
# MOST CONTROVERSIAL
# CALLS

### Nate Aaseng

Lerner Publications Company
Minneapolis

**page 1: Houston's Mike Renfro insists that he scored a touchdown, but his opinion isn't the one that counts! Instead it's up to the men in the striped shirts to untangle the snarl caused by Renfro's juggling act.**
**page 2: When the breaks don't go their way, players and fans alike are quick to point the finger at the "zebras."**

*To Doug and all those who called them as they see them*

Library of Congress Cataloging-in-Publication Data

Aaseng, Nathan.
    Football's most controversial calls.

    (Sports talk)
    Summary: Profiles eight National Football League games
in which the officials made controversial calls.
    1. Football—Officiating—Juvenile literature.
2. National Football League—Juvenile literature.
[1. National Football League—History. 2. Football—
History] I. Title. II. Series.
GV954.35.A22        1986        796.332'3        84-23329
ISBN 0-8225-1528-8 (lib. bdg.)

Manufactured in the United States of America

1  2  3  4  5  6  7  8  9  10  96  95  94  93  92  91  90  89  88  87  86

# ★★★ Contents ★★★

There's no pleasing everyone in this business. By calling it as he sees it,
this official has thrilled some fans—but outraged others.

# Introduction

Despite their eye-catching black-and-white shirts, football officials are almost invisible during football games; that is, until they make a call that fans don't like. When a game is running smoothly, the fans' attention is right where it belongs—on the players. But when a game is not going smoothly, officials often get far more attention than they want. At such times, it's as though they have suddenly run onto the field in gorilla suits!

For referees, attention usually means criticism, and most of them are quite used to being yelled at by fans, coaches, and players. They realize that this criticism is part of the job because every decision favors one team and goes against the other. Football officials know, too, that it's virtually impossible to officiate in the National Football League (NFL) without running into trouble at one time or another. In pro football, there are so many rules to enforce that seven officials are needed to keep order on the field. There are the referee, the umpire, the field judge, the back judge, the side judge, the head lineman, and the line judge. All have different responsibilities, and each one can run into a situation that calls for making a tough decision. As we shall see, there are times when an official is in for an argument, no matter what call he makes, because the simplest of rules can be full of hidden traps for the whistle-blower.

Controversial calls have played a key role in the history of pro football championships. Can you think of any other sport whose fans remember an official's call long after most of the game has been forgotten? As you read about some of the pitfalls that await pro football officials, you will see that an official's job is not for the weak of heart. You will also learn about some of the plays that have changed the rules of the game, have crowned the champions of the sport, and have sent millions of fans grumbling about how their team was "robbed!"

In 1981, this was one of the few games in which the Dallas Cowboys were outplayed.
And it was probably the only game in which they were outnumbered!

# ★★★ 1 ★★★

# The Cowboys Were Outnumbered

## *Dallas Cowboys vs. Detroit Lions*
### November 15, 1981

One of the most basic rules in sports is that each side must have an equal number of players. Even small children quickly catch on to that. So in the multi-million dollar business of pro football, is it possible for teams to actually get away with using an extra player at times? It may sound ridiculous, but it *has* happened. And it serves to show that the simplest rule can cause big problems for an official.

To understand how this problem could occur, think of the number of players involved in football. When the final seconds of a game are ticking off and the players are dashing in and out of the lineup, it takes a cool official to be able to sort out what's going on. At a quick glance, could *you* tell whether you were looking at 11 players or 12? On November 15, 1981, in Detroit's Silverdome,

some officials were put to the test on that question.

Although their record was only 4 and 6, the Detroit Lions were almost unbeatable at home and were still in the thick of their divisional race. Their opponents were the always-tough Dallas Cowboys, who had breezed through their schedule with an 8 and 2 mark.

The Cowboys wasted no time in taking command of the game. With quarterback Danny White throwing two touchdown passes to veteran wide receiver Drew Pearson, Dallas jumped out to a 17-0 lead. But then it was as if they had decided the game was already over, and they began to get careless. Detroit charged back in the second half, and, with star running back Billy Sims doing much of the work, they tied the score in the final quarter at 17 to 17.

The Cowboy offense shrugged their shoulders and got back to business. With typical Dallas precision, Danny White drove his team to a touchdown. Then with only 2:37 left to play, a 14-yard pass to tight end Jay Saldi put the Cowboys back on top.

Dallas had barely finished celebrating their score when Billy Sims outran all defenders to score from 81 yards away on a pass from Eric Hipple, and Detroit tied the game again. On their next possession, the stunned Cowboys were unable to answer the Detroit score, and they were forced to punt. With 1:13 left on the clock, Detroit started a drive of their own, and a pass to tight end David Hill brought them to within striking distance. After being temporarily sidetracked when Hipple was trapped for an 11-yard loss, Detroit moved into field-goal range. Reserve receiver Ulysses Norris caught a pass and ran to the Dallas 30-yard line.

As the clock ticked away to 10 seconds, the entire Detroit offense raced downfield. Since they had used up all of their time-outs, the Lions had only two

Although Dallas quarterback Danny White has mounted many exciting comebacks in his career, he could not arouse his slumbering offense against Detroit.

choices. They could try to get their offense set up quickly and toss an incomplete pass to stop the clock, allowing their placekicker plenty of time to set up a field-goal try. Or, they could try to set up for the field goal and hope to get the kick off before the last seconds.

With the deafening noise of the fans in the indoor stadium adding to the chaos, the Lions, unfortunately, started to do *both* plays at once! Players from their field-goal unit ran onto the field before the regular offense had left, and both groups were milling around the field, trying to figure out where they should line up. The Cowboys, meanwhile, were having almost as much trouble deciding which defensive unit to put on the field.

The Lions finally got their offense off the field and their kicking unit in place. Just as time was running out, placekicker Eddie Murray stepped forward and booted the ball toward the goalposts, 47 yards away. The kick could not have been better, and the Lions mobbed each other, thrilled with their 27 to 24 victory.

The Cowboys, however, were not so sure that the Lions had won the game. As they saw it, the group of Lions at the line of scrimmage seemed awfully large. If there had been an extra Detroit blocker on the field, it meant the Cowboys had not had a fair chance to block the kick.

Despite the Cowboys' heated protests, the officials allowed the kick and the resulting Detroit win to stand. But later photographs showed that the Cowboys' suspicions had been correct: there had been 12 Lions on the field at the time of the kick. In the confusion over which players should be on the field, one of the Lions' offensive players had failed to return to the sidelines.

The rulebook states that if there is an offensive penalty on the last play of the half, the down is *not* replayed. Therefore, had the extra player been spotted, the kick would have been disallowed, and the Lions would not have had a chance to try again. Then Detroit would have been penalized, and the contest would have gone into an overtime period.

Ignoring the game-ending chaos on the field, Detroit kicker Eddie Murray has eyes only for the ball.

But in the frantic finish, none of the seven officials had detected the extra blocker. No penalty had been called, and the game went into the record books as a Detroit win. Even when the violation was proved through photographs, it was too late to change the result, as it would simply be impossible to replay games every time that an undetected penalty was uncovered.

Fortunately, the outcome of the game made no difference in the play-off picture. Detroit missed the play-offs anyway while Dallas easily qualified, despite the loss. The game ended up as little more than a harmless oddity and a reminder to fans and officials that pro football can be so hectic at times that even seven officials can't always keep order.

## Number of Players

The game is to be played by two teams of 11 players each. If a snap or free kick is made while a team has more than 11 players on field, ball is in play and there is a five-yard penalty.

*Rule 5, Section 1, Article 1*

Billy Sims' electrifying run put the Cowboys on the ropes...

...and Eddie Murray finished them off.

When the dust settled on this game's final play, Dave Casper (87) had the ball in the end zone for the game-winning score. Afterwards, the NFL made sure such a bizarre play would never happen again.

# **2**

# **Fumbling Their Way to Victory**

## *Oakland Raiders vs. San Diego Chargers*
### September 10, 1978

Is it ever to an offensive team's advantage to fumble the ball on purpose and to put it up for grabs and risk giving it to the defensive team? Rarely anymore, thanks to a few wild seconds in San Deigo in 1978. In a game that looked more like soccer than football, there were so many shady, bizarre bounces on one play that league officials had to come up with a quick rule change to prevent such craziness from happening again. Unfortunately, the rule change came too late to help the officials who had to sort out the mess and declare a winner.

In an early-season contest that promised to be an interesting match, the powerful Oakland Raiders, finalists in the AFC (American Football Conference) title chase in the previous four years,

were going to test the rebuilt San Diego Chargers. The Chargers, once the sorriest group of athletes in the league, had come to life again. With an overwhelming young defensive line leading the way, they were eager to try their luck against their silver-and-black Western Division rivals.

San Diego fans got their money's worth that day. Oakland's quarterback, Ken Stabler, was in top form. Stabler passed for over 400 yards, and two of his receivers, All-Pro tight end Dave Casper and wide receiver Morris Bradshaw, each caught over 100 yards' worth of his passes. The Chargers' defense, however, had shut down the Raiders' strong running game, and San Diego held a 20-to-14 lead in the closing minutes.

Kenny "The Snake" Stabler made a career of beating opponents in the final minute of the game. But against the Chargers, the pinpoint magic that had made him one of the game's most accurate passers seemed to be failing him.

Then Stabler marched the Raiders downfield on a typical Oakland game-winning drive. But this time, the rally bogged down deep in San Diego territory. The Raiders had moved all the way to the Chargers' 14-yard line. But it was fourth down with only 10 seconds left in the game, and the Raiders were down to their final chance.

As they lined up, determined to sack Stabler and to end the game, San Diego's defensive line could feel victory close at hand. Stabler drifted back to pass and, finding no one open in the end zone, scrambled to his right. Suddenly, Chargers were pouring in on him from all directions. Blitzing linebacker Woodrow Lowe was the first to break through the blocking and rush in at Stabler.

As he was being pulled down by the Chargers, Stabler knew he had to somehow get rid of the ball, or the game would be lost. Just before he hit the ground, he either let the ball fall or tossed it forward. The ball tumbled toward the Charger goal line and began to slow down inside the 10-yard line.

Oakland's reserve running back, Peter Banaszak, reached the ball just ahead of the Chargers and scooped at it while running toward the goal line. But he failed to control the ball and fell out of the picture as the ball rolled even closer to the end zone.

Finally, Dave Casper arrived on the run from across the field. He bent down in midstride but struck the ball with his leg before he could pick it up, and the ball bounced into the end zone. The white-shirted Chargers had been unable to keep up with the bouncing ball, and Casper stumbled into the end zone ahead of them, falling on the ball.

San Diego fans were not quite certain what they had just witnessed, but it certainly did not look like football! And they were even more certain that there had *not* been a legal touchdown. But strange as it may seem, the officials ruled that there had been nothing illegal about the play, and they gave the Raiders a touchdown, which tied the score, 20-20. Seconds later, Oakland won the game by converting the extra point.

When the Raiders needed a sure-handed target, they called on Dave Casper. Fortunately for them, he could also be fumble-fingered on occasion!

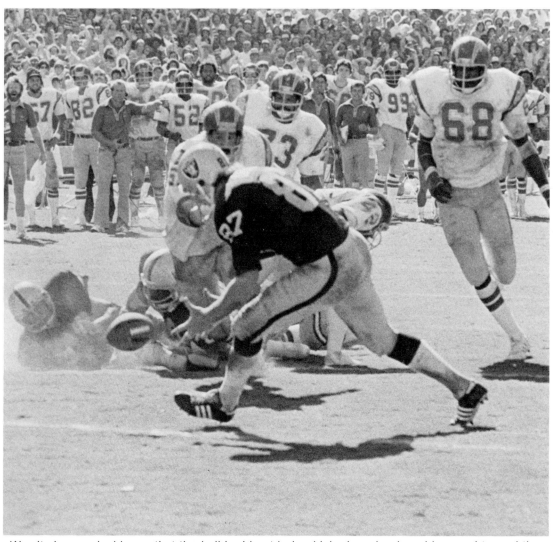

Was it sheer coincidence that the ball had kept being kicked, nudged, and bumped toward the goal line until Casper finally coralled it?

That win only served to brighten what had been a gloomy season for the Raiders, who didn't make the play-offs. But the Chargers, who missed the play-offs by one game, could not help but feel they had been robbed. Statements from the Oakland players after the game didn't help matters, either. The Raiders admitted to fumbling, batting, and kicking the ball forward on purpose, which, of course, wasn't legal. If Stabler had shoveled the ball forward, it should have been called an incomplete pass or intentional grounding. There were also rules against intentionally batting, shoving, or kicking the ball forward. The problem was how could the officials judge what a player was thinking? Was the man *trying* to knock the ball forward? Or was he honestly having trouble picking it up?

As a result of that confusion, the NFL quickly passed a new rule. Now on fourth-down or game-ending plays, only the player who fumbles the ball may recover it for the offense. Such a rule would have stopped Oakland from scoring on the play and would have cleared up a lot of problems for the officials.

Although the rule came too late for the Chargers, officials know that they won't have to worry about any more slapstick endings to football games.

---

### Intentional Fumble Forward

An intentional fumble forward is a forward pass.

*Rule 8, Section 1, Article 1*

### Fumble After Two-Minute Warning

After the two-minute warning, any fumble that occurs during a down, the fumbled ball may only be advanced by the offensive player who fumbled the ball, or any member of the defensive team.

*Rule 8, Section 4, Article 2*
NOTE: *This rule was added following the events described in this chapter.*

---

One way or another, Alan Page (88) tormented the Rams all afternoon.

# ★★★ 3 ★★★

# The Flinch That Shook Los Angeles

## *Los Angeles Rams vs. Minnesota Vikings*
### December 29, 1974

There may be no more obvious or embarrassing penalties in football than illegal motion and encroachment violations. Even a casual fan knows there is something wrong when one player charges ahead while everyone else is standing still. It is as glaring an error as leading a cavalry charge and finding that no one has followed you out of the fort!

Such a penalty seems so clear cut that it is hard to imagine how an official could get into trouble over it. Yet it was an ordinary illegal motion penalty that had the Los Angeles Rams fuming in 1974. And to make matters even more uncomfortable for the officials, the penalty happened in the NFC title game.

Two defensive-minded teams, the Rams and the Minnesota Vikings, were pounding away at each other on a cold Minnesota Sunday. For most of the game, the offensive units served as punching bags for the stronger defensive players. By the middle of the third quarter, the score was only 7 to 3 in favor of the Vikings.

When Minnesota punter Mike Eischied pinned the Rams back on their 1-yard line with a beautifully placed punt, the Rams' situation looked grim. The Viking fans howled, hoping to see the Rams dumped in their own end zone. Instead, Los Angeles wriggled out to their 25-yard line.

The Vikings then guessed that a pass was coming, and they sent their linebackers blitzing after Ram quarterback James Harris. Harris barely had time to set up for the pass when he was engulfed by Jeff Siemon and Roy Winston. Somehow the quarterback slipped away from those two and spotted wide receiver Harold Jackson open far downfield.

By the time of this third quarter fumble, Ram quarterback James Harris must have suspected that this wasn't going to be his day.

Harris tossed the ball to Jackson, and the speedy receiver raced downfield toward the end zone. Only safety Jeff Wright had a slim chance of heading Jackson off before he scored, and Wright bumped him out of bounds at the 2-yard line.

It was a fine defensive play, but it seemed like a wasted effort. With a first down on the 2 following that 73-yard pass, it seemed a sure bet that Los Angeles would score the go-ahead touchdown. It appeared even more certain when running back John Cappelletti carried the ball to within six inches of the goal line on the first down.

Now the Vikings dug in for their goal-line stand, stacking six large defensive linemen in front of the Ram blockers. All-Pro tackle Alan Page found himself on the right side of the Viking line across from two of the Rams' best blockers, Tom Mack and Charlie Cowen. The teams lined up, poised for an all-out effort in this crucial situation. Suddenly, a lone player in a purple shirt broke from his stance like a sprinter charging out of the starting blocks. It was Page. He barged into Mack and

Cowan before the ball was snapped, and the play was blown dead before it started.

What seemed like a simple case of encroachment against Page was quickly clouded when Page immediately pointed an accusing finger at the Ram linemen. Page claimed that he was drawn offside when one of the Ram linemen moved from his set position. If that were the case, the Rams would have to be penalized five yards for illegal motion. Page later explained that he saw one of the Rams "flinch." That may seem like a very minor movement, but once an offensive lineman takes his stance, even flinching is not allowed. The back judge supported Page's claim and ordered the Rams to move back five yards from the line of scrimmage. Officially, Tom Mack was the Ram charged with the mistake.

Mack could hardly believe what had happened to him. He insisted that he had not so much as blinked before Page charged. Teammate Cowan argued hotly in Mack's defense, convinced that Page was pulling a fast one on the officials. The call, however, still went against the Rams.

Alan Page

James Harris

Faced with a second down and over five yards to go instead of second down and inches, the Rams had to switch tactics. Rather than blast straight ahead, they went to a roll-out option. Harris swung to his right and gained back three of the lost yards before he was tackled at the 2. On the third down, he tried a similar roll-out. As the Vikings came up

to tackle him this time, he flipped the ball towards a receiver in the end zone. Minnesota's Jackie Wallace barely got a hand on the pass and tipped it off course. It fluttered into the hands of Viking linebacker Wally Hilgenberg for an interception.

The Rams had advanced the ball against Minnesota as far as a team could go without scoring, but the 99-yard drive earned them nothing on the scoreboard. Due to the illegal motion penalty against Mack, an almost certain touchdown had been lost. That missed opportunity came back to haunt the Rams when they lost the game by only four points, 14 to 10. Very likely, the call had cost them the game, the NFC championship, and a trip to the Super Bowl.

Although he has looked at films of the play over a hundred times, Mack says he has yet to see any motion on his part. There were two people, however, who were convinced that Mack had moved, and one of those people was an official. Unfortunately for Mack, the official's opinion was the one that counted.

### Encroaching
A player is Encroaching on the neutral zone when any part of his body is in it at the snap.
*Rule 3, Section 20*

### Encroachment and Offside
Penalty: For encroaching or being offside: Loss of five yards from previous spot....
*Rule 7, Section 2, Article 2*

### Player Movement at Snap
At the snap, all offensive players must be stationary in their positions: without any movement of feet, head or arms; without swaying of body....
Penalty: For player illegally in motion at snap: Loss of five yards from previous spot. In case of doubt, this penalty shall be enforced.
*Rule 7, Section 2, Article 5*

Kenny Stabler rolls into the end zone to score the game-winning touchdown. According to New England's Ray Hamilton, Stabler had barely been touched on the roughing call that had given the Raiders their final chance.

# 4

# Could He Help It?

*New England Patriots vs. Oakland Raiders*
December 18, 1976

When a quarterback goes back to pass, he's a sitting duck. He is often a small player who stands looking for an open receiver while huge linemen try to fight their way through blockers to knock him down. The passer is vulnerable and valuable and often needs more protection than his blockers can give him. So quarterbacks count on a second line of defense from the officials, who have the important task of seeing that the quarterback doesn't get more punishment than the rules allow.

The rules about quarterback protection have not always been clear. As it stands now, the quarterback is fair game for all tacklers as long as he has the ball. The problem comes when he is hit just *after* he releases the ball. If a pass rusher has built up such speed that he can't help hitting the quarterback, no penalty is called. But a referee must be an expert in the laws of physics to calculate whether or not a pass rusher could have avoided contact.

One such roughing-the-passer call helped crown a Super Bowl champ and put much of New England in an uproar. It happened during the first round of the 1976 play-off contest. The New England Patriots, who had improved their record from 3 and 11 in 1975 to 11 and 3, were the surprise entry in the play-offs. Their opponents, the Oakland Raiders, had posted the best record in the NFL with a 13 and 1 mark.

The Raiders had good reason to worry about the Patriots, however. Oakland's only loss during the season had been to New England when they had been destroyed, 48 to 17. The Raiders had returned home muttering about New England's "seven-man line." The Patriots not only boasted five strong offensive

27

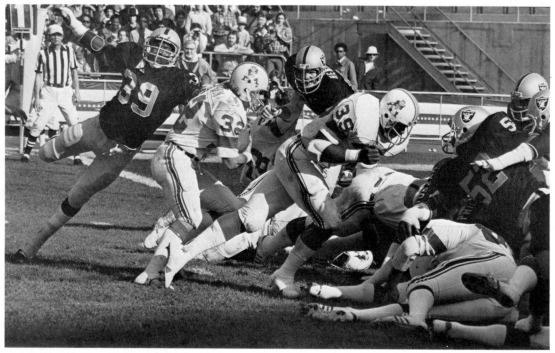

As Patriot fullback Sam "Bang" Cunningham (39) blasts a path into the end zone, teammate Andy Johnson (32) escapes Willie Hall (left).

linemen; they also received great blocking from both tight end Russ Francis and fullback Sam "Bam" Cunningham, who could block as well as any lineman.

In the first half of the play-off game, New England picked up where they had left off in their previous meeting with the Raiders. Their blockers cleared the way for runners on a long scoring drive, and Andy Johnson put the finishing touches on the march with a one-yard burst into the end zone.

The Raiders answered with some offensive power of their own when quarterback Ken Stabler led Oakland back to the lead before halftime. He first set up a field goal, and then he threw a scoring pass to veteran Fred Biletnikoff for a 10-to-7 edge.

New England took control again in the second half when Francis broke free from the rough Raider defensive backs to score on a 31-yard pass catch. Shortly after, Jess Phillips followed with a three-yard touchdown run behind his friendly wall of blockers.

Late in the game, Oakland fullback Mark van Eeghen closed the gap to 21-17 with a one-yard plunge, but it appeared to be too little too late. New England started to use up the clock as they moved in for the game-winning score, but a costly offside on a third-and-one situation hurt their chances, and an official's error made things even worse. None of the men in the striped shirts had spotted the illegal holding by Oakland against Russ Francis on a crucial pass play. With 4:12 left, the ball went back to the Raiders.

That was plenty of time for Stabler to score, and he calmly directed his team toward the Patriots' end zone. In fact, he was almost *too* careless with his time, for only a minute and a half remained when his reliable tight end, Dave Casper, caught a pass for 21 yards to the New England 14. There the New England defensive line regrouped for a final all-out effort. Mel Lunsford blunted the Oakland rally by sacking Stabler for an 8-yard loss. Next, Stabler tried to go back to his ace, Casper, but the pass fell incomplete.

Now it was third down and 18 from the 22, and only 57 seconds remained. With the score 21 to 17, Oakland *had* to have a touchdown; a field goal would not be enough. Stabler went back to pass once more, but with Patriots breaking through the black-shirted wall of Raider blockers, he was again forced into throwing incomplete. Just after the pass left his hand, he was bumped by New England tackle Ray "Sugar Bear" Hamilton.

Oakland's desperate fourth-and-18 situation was instantly changed as a yellow flag fluttered to the turf. Not only was a 15-yard penalty marked off against New England, but the Raiders were also entitled to an automatic first down. The officials ruled that Hamilton had roughed the passer.

Hamilton and the rest of the Patriots howled in disbelief. They claimed that Hamilton had built up such speed while rushing Stabler that he could not have avoided running into the quarterback. If that were the case, the referee should have waved off the collision as "incidental contact." That sort of thing happened all the time; it had probably happened to New England's quarterback half a dozen times in that very game.

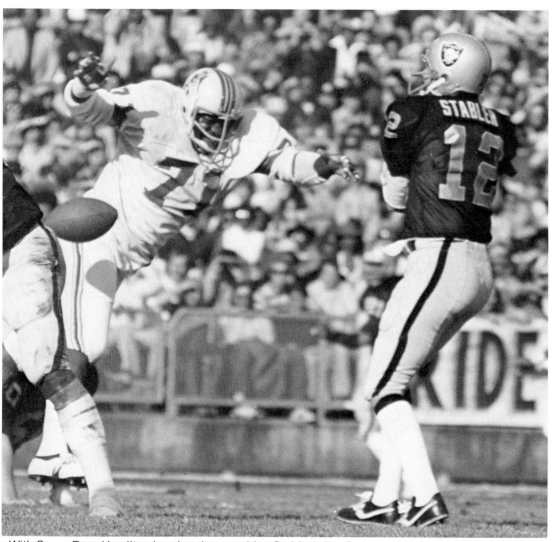

With Sugar Bear Hamilton bearing down on him, Stabler's hurried pass falls incomplete. A fraction of a second later, Hamilton plowed into the quarterback.

Ray "Sugar Bear" Hamilton

the grateful Raiders easily scored the winning touchdown with Stabler trotting in around his left end. Oakland went on to thrash the Pittsburgh Steelers, 24 to 7, in the AFC championship and then beat the Minnesota Vikings, 32 to 14, in Super Bowl XI.

A close call by the officials had made the Raiders' win possible. New England could only wonder what would have happened if the officials had interpreted the roughing rule a little differently. Would *they* have been the Super Bowl champs?

### Roughing Passer
A player of the defensive team shall not run into a passer after the ball has left his hand. Penalty: For running into the passer: Loss of 15 yards from the previous spot, and disqualification when flagrant.
*Rule 12, Section 2, Article 11*

### Quicker Whistle
The referee must determine whether an opponent had a reasonable chance to stop his momentum during an attempt to block or bat a pass or to tackle the passer while he was still in possession.
*Rule 12, Section 2, Article 11*

The Patriots couldn't believe that their tremendous effort and their championship hopes would be ruined by such a borderline call.

The referee, however, stuck to his ruling that Hamilton had not made enough of an effort to avoid hurting Stabler. The furious Patriots stormed around the field and argued so long that they were penalized further for unsportsmanlike conduct!

Aided by so much penalty yardage,

In his attempt to block this overtime field goal by Green Bay's Don Chandler,
a Colt (75) gives the first signal that the kick is good!

# 5

# Why the Uprights Are So High

*Baltimore Colts vs. Green Bay Packers*
December 26, 1965

For more than 40 years, the uprights on football goalposts stood only 10 feet high. Then in 1966, they were raised to 20 feet. This was done so that officials would not have to guess if a very high kick had stayed inside an imaginary line above the post. As is often the case, it took a dramatic and bizarre incident to bring about the rule change. And for Baltimore Colt fans and a crew of officials, the change came too late.

The year was 1965. The Baltimore Colts and the Green Bay Packers had tied for first place in the Western Conference of the NFL, and a play-off game was held in Green Bay to determine which team would face the Cleveland Browns for the league title. Baltimore went into the game with a huge disadvantage. Star quarterback Johnny Unitas was unable to play due to injuries, and his backup, Gary Cuozzo, was also out of action. As a result, the Colts had gone to a makeshift offense with halfback Tom Matte gamely trying to fill the quarterback spot.

After the first Packer offensive series, however, the quarterback situation evened up a little. Green Bay's Bart Starr threw a pass to Bill Anderson, who fumbled when hit by a jarring tackle. Baltimore's Don Shinnick picked up the loose ball and returned it for a touchdown. In an attempt to stop Shinnick, Starr had been injured, and he, too, was forced to sit out the game. At the way things were going, Bart's backup, Zeke Bratkowski, must have wondered about *his* chances of surviving the game!

Equipped with a wristband full of Colt offensive plays, Baltimore's volunteer quarterback, Tom Matte, gets last-minute advice from Coach Don Shula.

Meanwhile, Colt quarterbacks Gary Cuozzo (above) and John Unitas watched helplessly.

In the second half, the Packers finally got on the scoreboard on a one-yard run by halfback Paul Hornung. Baltimore's offense could do little against Green Bay without a decent passing attack, so it was up to the Colt defense to hang onto the narrow lead.

Although the Colt defenders fought grimly, luck was not on their side. Thanks to a disputed roughing call on lineman Billy Ray Smith, Green Bay moved into Baltimore territory. As the clock wound down to two minutes in the final quarter, the Packers stormed inside the Baltimore 20-yard line. As had happened so often that day, however, they were unable to take advantage of the touchdown opportunity. With 1:58 left to play, Baltimore stopped them on third down, and Green Bay was forced to go for the tie with a field goal.

Without their regular quarterbacks to take charge, both teams sputtered on offense. Bratkowski was able to move his team far better than the Colts' Matte was, and the Packers gained more than twice as many first downs. But whenever the Packers got near scoring territory, their attack stalled, and they were unable to score. At halftime, the Colts held a 10 to 0 lead.

Don Chandler was an excellent veteran placekicker. With the goalposts only 22 yards from where the ball would be spotted, it seemed like a routine kick. Chandler was about as likely to miss as a pro baseball player is to drop a pop fly, and he concentrated totally on the ball as his holder set it on the ground.

Don Chandler needed a high kick—too high for the officials' comfort—to launch the ball past a forest of Colt arms. Bart Starr (l5) shrugged off his injuries long enough to spot the ball for Chandler.

Quickly, Chandler stepped forward and swung his leg. As soon as he struck the ball, he knew that he had not connected as well as he had hoped. The ball sailed high in the air and would easily be long enough, but it also veered dangerously close to the right upright. As it soared high above the post, it came so close that it was difficult to tell whether or not the kick was good.

Standing back in the end zone, the field judge took a long look as the ball flew past. Then he raised his arms over his head. The kick was good, and the game was now tied. But that was not the way the Colts saw it. Baltimore placekicker Lou Michaels claimed the kick was a good three feet wide, and other Colt defenders standing near Chandler echoed that opinion.

It was not unusual, of course, for the Colts to protest a close decision that went against them. But what really put the officials on the spot was a simple facial expression. That expression belonged to Chandler. After kicking the ball and seeing where it was headed, the Green Bay kicker had looked like a man who had just dropped his wallet in the ocean! He winced, and his shoulders slumped as he shook his head in disgust. That was hardly the reaction you would expect from someone who had just made a pressure-filled kick to tie a championship game. It was obvious that even Chandler thought he had blown the kick.

Although the officials believed they had called the play correctly, there was no way they would ever convince the Colts that they had not been robbed of the championship. Green Bay went on to win the game, 13 to 10, when Chandler kicked another short field goal late in overtime. At least there was no doubt about whether or not the game-winning kick was good.

The simple solution to the problem of judging field goals was to lengthen the uprights. Over the past few years, a good number of place kicks in the NFL have struck one upright or another. Each time it happens, the officials can thank Don Chandler. Since the uprights were raised, there are rarely any disputes about field goals, which is one less headache for a harried official.

---

**Goal Posts**
All goal posts will be the single-standard type, offset from the end line and bright gold in color. The uprights will extend 30 feet above the crossbar....
*Rule 1, Section 3*
NOTE: *The rule about 30-foot goalposts was added following the events described in this chapter.*

---

"We're Number One!" exclaims Terry Bradshaw, after sweating out a narrow victory. Although it's nice to be good, Bradshaw knows it doesn't hurt to be lucky, too.

# ★★★ 6 ★★★

# Interference!

## *Dallas Cowboys vs. Pittsburgh Steelers*
### January 21, 1979

Pass interference is a prime example of what is known as a judgment call. Two qualified observers standing ear to ear can watch the same play; one will call pass interference while the other will not. The problem is that both the offensive and defensive players have a right to try to catch the ball. If either interferes with an opponent while the ball is in the air, it is a penalty. On frequent occasions when two or more players collide going for the ball, it is up to the official to decide if one of them bumped the other out of the way.

If two neutral observers can disagree about pass interference, imagine how two very competitive teams would react to an official's call! It is not surprising that, except for the most flagrant fouls, pass interference calls almost always draw arguments from the two teams involved.

Sometimes teams complain that pass interference should have been called when it was not. The most notable case was the "Hail, Mary" pass that Dallas completed to shock Minnesota in the 1975 play-offs. Many insisted that Dallas receiver Drew Pearson pushed off on defender Nate Wright on the winning play. But the most controversial pass interference call occurred in Super Bowl XIII in 1979.

That year, the Dallas Cowboys and the Pittsburgh Steelers were by far the best teams in their conferences. Dallas had entered the Super Bowl fresh from a 28 to 0 pummeling of the Los Angeles Rams, and the Pittsburgh Steelers had clobbered Houston, 34 to 5. Super Bowls are also supposed to use the NFL's top officials, so one would not expect many problems with the officiating.

While Terry Bradshaw is preoccupied with Thomas Henderson, Mike Hegman relieves him of the ball and scores a touchdown that sparked a first-half Cowboy rally.

The first half of the game was smoothly played and exciting. Pittsburgh's Terry Bradshaw saw that he could not run against the Cowboys' flex defense, so he took to the air instead. Over the first two quarters of play, his wide receivers, John Stallworth and Lynn Swann, outran and outjumped the entire Dallas defensive backfield. Bradshaw fired three touchdown passes in the first half, two to Stallworth and one to running back Rocky Bleier. Then the Cowboys took to the air to score a touchdown of their own when linebacker Mike Hegman stole the ball from Bradshaw and ran for 37 yards.

Dallas fired up in the second half to overcome the 21-to-14 lead. The Cowboys marched deep into Steeler territory, only to miss an easy touchdown when Jackie Smith dropped a sure touchdown pass. They did get a field goal, however, and cut the lead to 21-17.

The Steelers then struggled to work the ball out of their own end of the field. With their running attack still bogged down, they were lucky to reach their 45. It was second down and 5, and Bradshaw decided it was time to try a long pass to Lynn Swann. Swann had been a good bet so far, grabbing five passes for a total of 102 yards.

Since they had bottled up the running plays so well, Dallas was expecting the Steelers to pass. Safety Cliff Harris charged in on a blitz and forced Bradshaw to hurry his throw. This happened to be one of the few times in the game that Swann was perfectly covered by Cowboy cornerback Benny Barnes. Barnes matched him stride for stride and held his position to the inside of the field as the ball sailed downfield.

Both men looked back and saw that Bradshaw had desperately thrown the ball up for grabs. The pass was short and was headed toward the inside of the field. Barnes was closer to the ball than Swann was, and he slowed down to try for the interception. Swann, meanwhile, tried to cut back to the inside. The two collided, and Swann tripped over Barnes' legs at the Dallas 23.

The ball fell to the ground untouched, and an official watching from just a few feet away signaled an incomplete pass. In his judgment, the contact had been accidental. But the field judge, who was further away, decided that he had seen a penalty and pulled out his flag.

Who tripped whom? His legs tangled up with Benny Barnes (31), Lynn Swann (88) watches the pass drop out of reach.

Both Swann and Barnes were pleased to see the penalty flag because each was convinced that the other had committed the foul. So when the penalty was marked off against Dallas, the Cowboys were furious! In their view, they had just seen Swann push Barnes, who fell, and Swann had then tripped over Barnes. But the field judge stood by his call. The result was a costly 33-yard penalty against Dallas, and the Steelers had a first down on the Dallas 23.

Four plays later, Pittsburgh finally found a running play that worked when Franco Harris bolted 22 yards up the middle on a trap play for a touchdown.

Cowboy Aaron Kyle (25) wants to know what that penalty flag is doing on the ground. Benny Barnes (31), meanwhile, was happy to see it thrown—until he discovered the penalty was not on Pittsburgh but on him!

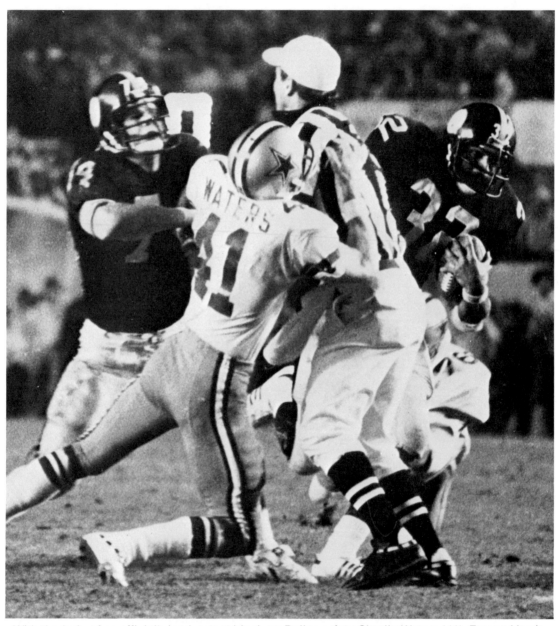

With the help of an official's inadvertant block on Dallas safety Charlie Waters (41), Franco Harris (32) found clear sailing to the end zone for a fourth-quarter touchdown.

Ironically, the Cowboys were again done in by an official. During the play, one of the whistle-blowers had unwittingly gotten between Harris and Cowboy safety Charlie Waters, preventing Waters from making the tackle. Pittsburgh was suddenly ahead, 28 to 17.

Pittsburgh then kicked off, and the wobbly kick was fumbled by the Dallas blockers. The Steelers recovered and scored one play later on a leaping touchdown catch by Swann. That made the score 35 to 17, which seemed to put the game well out of the Cowboys' reach. Dallas scared the Steelers with a frantic rally in the closing minutes, but time ran out on them, and Pittsburgh won, 35 to 31.

It was small comfort when Barnes reported that he had received an apology from the NFL front office. They had agreed that pass interference should not have been called on him. But right or wrong, the call had *already* changed the game, and the Cowboys had lost. The 33-yard penalty is still in the record books, and the Steelers are still wearing their 1979 Super Bowl rings.

### Pass Interference by Either Team

It is pass interference by either team when any player movement beyond the offensive line hinders the progress of an eligible opponent in his attempt to reach a pass, except such incidental movement or contact which may occur when two or more eligible players make a simultaneous and bona fide attempt to catch or bat the ball....
*Rule 8, Section 2, Article 5*

### Simultaneous and Bona Fide Attempt

...Any bodily contact, however severe, between players who are making a simultaneous and bona fide attempt to catch or bat ball is not interference.
*Rule 8, Section 2, Article 5*

Any eligible player looking for and intent on playing the ball who initiates contact, however severe, while attempting to move to the spot of completion or interception will not be called for interference.
*1985 Rule Clarification*

Find the ball in this picture. Can't do it? Neither could the officals,
and the Raiders believed that cost them the game.

# ★★★7★★★

# Keep Your Eye on the Ball!

## *Oakland Raiders vs. Denver Broncos*
### January 1, 1978

The advice, "Keep your eye on the ball," is usually given to baseball players and golfers. But it is also sound advice for football officials and advice that is *not* as easy to follow as it sounds. Quarterbacks, for instance, are experts at faking handoffs and passes that fool defenders and television camera people as well as officials. Huge ex-lineman Bubba Smith often tells the tall tale of how he used to tackle an entire backfield and throw people out until he found the player who had the ball!

The outcome of a football game often depends on the officials knowing where the ball is at all times, and many important games have hinged on whether or not an official saw a fumble occur before the ball carrier was tackled. One of the most dramatic of these situations took place in the 1977 AFC championship game, the first championship

contest ever for the Denver Broncos.

The Broncos were playing at home against their archrivals, the Oakland Raiders. Oakland, the wild-card team, had finished one game behind Denver's 12 and 2 mark. The teams had split their two games in the regular season, each winning comfortably on the other's home turf. This championship game was billed as a match between Oakland's powerful offense and Denver's great defense.

Oakland started the game with a typical Raider strategy. They sent rugged, sure-handed backs like Mark van Eeghan behind a wall of All-Pro blockers —tackle Art Shell, guard Gene Upshaw, and tight end Dave Casper—who provided 800 pounds of bulk on the left side. The Raiders pushed around the Broncos' fine defense on two long drives, but, unfortunately, moved the entire

Haven Moses

ver recovered on the Raider 17. Then a quick pass from quarterback Craig Morton to tight end Riley Odoms gave Denver a first down on the 2. The Bronco fans rocked the stadium as their team threatened to open up a comfortable lead. If the Broncos could score, they were certain that their Orange Crush defense could protect a 14-to-3 lead.

Hoping to muscle their way into the end zone, Denver sent running back Rob Lytle into the line. But Lytle ran into a jarring tackle by Raider safety Jack Tatum near the line of scrimmage. Lytle could not hang onto the ball, and it fell to the ground. Oakland's Mike McCoy alertly spotted the fumble and recovered it. It was just the break that Oakland needed to get out of deep trouble.

But the head lineman saw the play differently. He spotted the ball at the two-yard line and signaled that it belonged to Denver. The Broncos' were dumbfounded. They did not think there could be any doubt on the play. But the officials had not seen the fumble and had declared Lytle tackled at the two. He believed the fumble had happened after Lytle had gone down.

length of the field twice without scoring a touchdown. Instead, they had to settle for field goals both times and made only one of them for a 3 to 0 lead. All of this effort was wiped out in a few seconds, however, when Denver's wide receiver, Haven Moses, slipped past a defender and ran 74 yards for a touchdown and a 7-to-3 halftime lead.

In the third quarter, Oakland committed another grave error. Running back Clarence Davis fumbled, and Den-

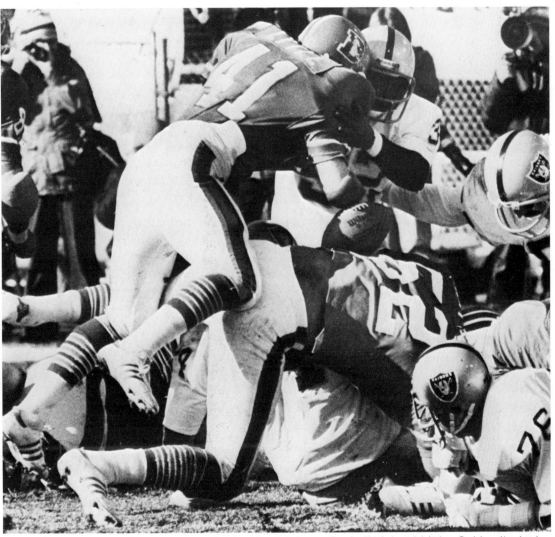

Rob Lytle's feet are still churning, but he doesn't have the ball. A hard hit by Oakland's Jack Tatum had jarred it loose.

As is often the case on controversial plays, the penalized team was further penalized for their heated outcry over the injustice. The ball was placed on the one-yard line, half the distance from the original line of scrimmage. Denver then called a play that Oakland did not expect. Quarterback Morton, who had such a sore hip that he had been hospitalized most of the week, took off running to the right side. The Raiders closed in to tackle him. But as they did, Morton pitched the ball to fullback John Keyworth. John scored easily, making the score 14 to 3.

The lead turned out to be less safe than the Denver fans had thought, however. With Stabler passing to the remarkable Dave Casper, Oakland scored two more touchdowns before the final gun. But Denver's offense was able to come up with six more points, and they used up the clock with running plays to keep Oakland from getting one last scoring chance. The Broncos held on to win by a score of 20 to 17. In the eyes of the Raiders, the officials had given Denver a touchdown and the margin of victory.

The fact that this is the third chapter involving the Raiders brings up an important point. Even though an official's call may have an important effect on a game, sooner or later the breaks start to even out. Earlier we've seen two examples of how the Raiders benefitted from some clouded calls. This time, they were on the other end. The no-fumble call may not have been totally responsible for putting the defending Super Bowl champs from Oakland out of the play-offs, but it certainly helped. Now it was Denver's turn to feel grateful as they won their first AFC title.

---

**Dead Ball**
An official shall declare dead ball and the down ended:
(b) when a runner is so held or otherwise restrained that this forward progress end.
(c) when a runner is contacted by a defensive player and he touches the ground with any part of his body except his hands or feet....
(m) when any official signals dead ball or sounds his whistle, even though inadvertantly.
*Rule 7, Section 4, Article 1*

---

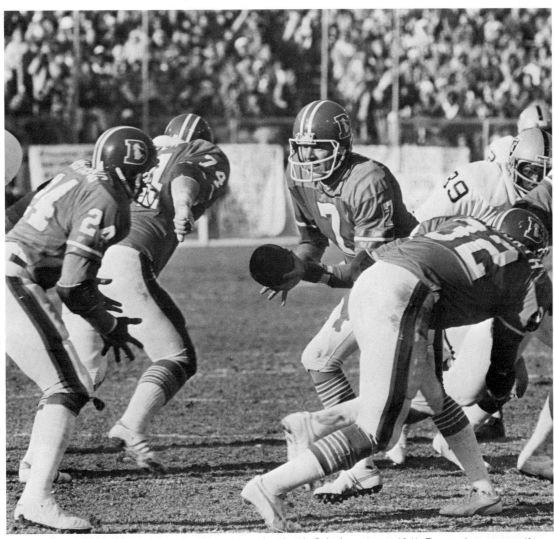

Led by quarterback Craig Morton (7) and running back Otis Armstrong (24), Denver's conservative grind-it-out defense helped to give them an important win over the Raiders—and their first AFC title.

The Steel Curtain, in the person of L. C. Greenwood (68), falls on quarterback Dan Pastorini.

# ★★★ 8 ★★★

# The Edge of Indecision

## *Houston Oilers vs. Pittsburgh Steelers*
### January 6, 1980

When you realize how much an official's decision can affect the outcome of a championship football game, you get an idea of how much pressure football's "zebras" are under. They want to be absolutely certain of a call before throwing the flag. But, as a team of officials found out in the 1979 AFC championship game, they had better not think about the call *too* long before making a decision. That incident involved the question of whether or not a receiver had control of the ball before it went out of bounds.

Thanks to television's instant replay, the in-bounds/out-of-bounds question is always a potentially embarrassing problem for officials. They have a split second to decide if both of the receiver's feet were in bounds at the time of the catch and also if he had the ball firmly in his grasp before stepping out. After

the official has made the call, the replay can slow down the action, and people can see whether or not the call was right.

The game was a hard-fought title contest between Central Division rivals Houston and Pittsburgh. The Oilers stunned the defending champion Steelers early when Vernon Perry picked off a Pittsburgh pass and ran it back for a touchdown. As the Steelers slowly battled back against the grudging Oiler defense, they were often forced into difficult third-down situations. But somehow they came up with the yards that were needed to keep their drives going.

Meanwhile, Houston's power offense was stopped cold. The Oilers relied heavily on big running back Earl Campbell to carry the ball downfield. But Earl was hurting from injuries when the game started, and he felt even worse as

**53**

the game went on. The Steelers, knowing that Houston's deep pass threat, Ken Burrough, was out of action, concentrated on stopping Campbell. Earl was tackled after receiving handoffs several times during the first half and had gained only two yards by halftime.

With Houston's offense paralyzed, the Steelers began to take control of the game. They had evened the score by the half, and they moved ahead when John Stallworth caught a 20-yard scoring pass in the third period. With the score at 17 to 10 in favor of Pittsburgh, the Steelers pinned the Oilers deep in their end of the field with a punt. It seemed as though Pittsburgh was ready to finish off Houston.

Oiler quarterback Dan Pastorini, however, finally turned to the pass and moved his team down the length of the field, drawing within striking range with a first down on the Steeler six-yard line. Pastorini called his play in the huddle and then stood behind his center. One glance at the defense gave him the queasy feeling that Pittsburgh was going to blitz from all sides. Just before the hike, Pastorini quickly called a change of play at the line of scrimmage.

As expected, the Steelers roared in after Pastorini. Dan only had time to drop back two frantic steps and loft a pass to the right corner of the end zone. His teammate, Mike Renfro, ran after it with Steeler cornerback Ron Johnson staring him in the eye. The Oiler receiver pried loose from Johnson just long enough to reach out for the ball and pull it into his body before stumbling out of the end zone. Houston fans were already celebrating the touchdown, but a couple of questions had to be cleared up first. Were Renfro's feet in bounds? And did he have control of the ball while in bounds?

The side judge was the man responsible for making the decision. Both teams looked to him for the call, ready to cheer if the call went their way or to argue if it did not. But for a while, they could do neither. It seemed that finally there had been a play that was too close to call. The side judge looked to some of the other officials for help in making his decision, but none of them felt they had seen the play clearly enough to offer an opinion.

Pastorini had laid a perfect pass just beyond the reach of Ron Johnson (29) to Mike Renfro in the back corner of the end zone.

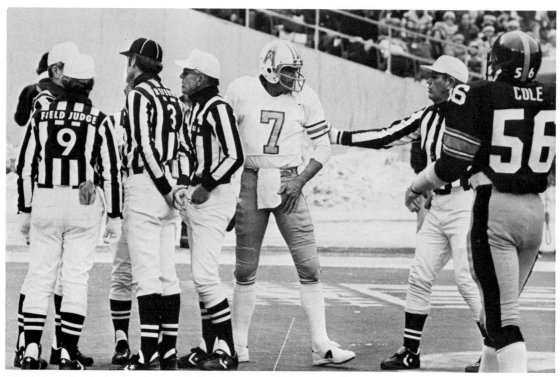

This is going to be hard enough to figure out without Dan Pastorini's help, decides one official, as the others try to nail down just what happened on Renfro's catch.

As the puzzled players and fans looked on, the officials went into a huddle. They still had not given an indication of whether it had been a touchdown or an incomplete pass. Finally, they broke their huddle and came out with news that crushed the Oilers: No touchdown.

While order was being restored, the television network broadcast the slow-motion replays. Renfro's feet were shown to be clearly in bounds, and the commentators wondered aloud if the Oilers had been robbed. The fuming Oilers had to settle for a field goal, which only cut the lead to 17-13. The decision seemed to affect the Oiler defense, who gave up 10 fourth-quarter points to give Pittsburgh a 27-to-13 victory.

When the game was over, the Renfro play was on everyone's mind, including the Steelers'. They griped that the indecision on the call had cast doubt as to whether they really deserved to win the game and be champions of the AFC. That one incomplete pass grabbed the headlines and spoiled an otherwise remarkable effort by both teams.

The explanation finally given was that Renfro did *not* have control of the ball when he stepped out of bounds. Skeptical Oilers then asked why the usual sign for bobbling the ball out of bounds had not been given immediately.

When films of the play taken from a variety of angles were examined, it truly turned out to be a tough call. From some camera shots, it appeared that Renfro was juggling the ball as he went out of bounds; in others, it looked as if Renfro had control of the ball. A roomful of reporters was shown the play from six different angles and asked to decide whether or not it should have been a touchdown. Although a slim majority thought it was a touchdown, the reporters couldn't reach an agreement, either.

In the end, it was not the final call that had caused the biggest problem. The play was so close that, no matter which way it had been called, one team would have claimed to have been robbed.

Then the controversy was multiplied by the officials' hesitation in making the call. To the Oilers, it seemed to indicate that the officials didn't know what had happened or that they were hesitant to make a close call that went against the home fans. Officials are paid to make decisions, and that incident showed that any decision is better than none, even when a play is "too close to call."

---

### Player Possession

...In order for an eligible receiver of a forward pass to be in possession, he must control the ball throughout the act of clearly touching both feet, or any other part of his body other than his hands, to the ground inbounds....

*Rule 3, Section 2, Article 6*

---

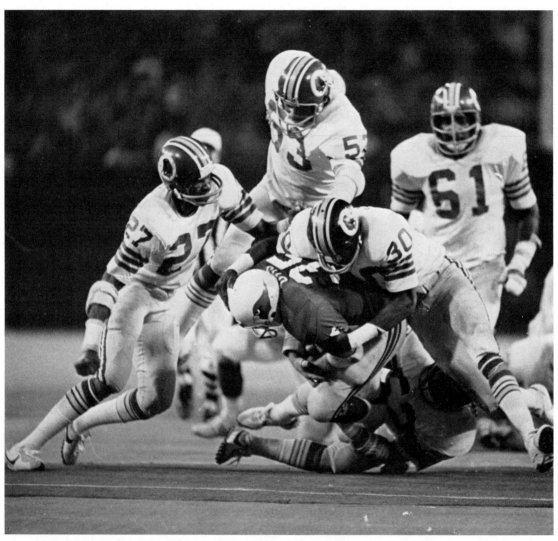

The Redskins think they should be in the showers enjoying a hard-fought win instead of working overtime to stop the Cardinals' husky fullback, Jim Otis.

# ★★★ 9 ★★★
# How Long Is Long Enough?

*Washington Redskins vs. St. Louis Cardinals*
November 16, 1975

No matter where they occur, pass receptions can cause trouble for officials. Passes down the middle of the field can be just as tricky to call as sideline passes. In fact, one of the most uncomfortable moments for football officials came on a high pass in the middle of the end zone. Although several officials had a good view of the entire play, it still took a lot of discussion to answer a simple question: Did the player catch the ball?

That event happened on November 16, 1975, in St. Louis when two evenly matched rivals from the NFC's Eastern Division were meeting in an important game. Both the St. Louis Cardinals and the Washington Redskins had finished with 10 wins and 4 losses the year before, and both were 6 and 2 going into this game.

Washington had won an earlier meeting between the teams, 27 to 17. They began this game as if they would repeat that result when they stopped the Cardinals' highly rated offense and produced a pair of touchdowns of their own. By the end of the third period, the Cardinals still had not figured out how to beat the Redskins and trailed, 14 to 3.

But St. Louis wasn't called the Cardiac Cards for nothing. They had a habit of pulling out wins in the final seconds, and now they looked as though they might do it again. The Cards scored a touchdown, and, following a Redskin field goal, started their march downfield. But they were cutting it even closer than usual when they still trailed by seven with 20 seconds to go. With the ball on the Redskin 6, the Cardinals were down to their final play.

Enjoying the best pass protection in football, St. Louis quarterback Jim Hart could wait patiently...

Looking for speedy wide reciever Mel Gray, quarterback Jim Hart dropped back to pass. Gray was a long-ball specialist, the kind of receiver who is usually not as effective in close quarters near the end zone. But using his speed to keep free from Washington defenders, he raced into the middle of the end zone. Hart fired the pass, and the 5-foot, 9-inch Gray leaped into the air to grab it. Almost as soon as Gray got his hands on the ball, Washington's excellent safety, Ken Houston, closed in on him. Houston hit Gray solidly with a tackle, and the ball popped out of the receiver's grasp and bounced harmlessly into the end zone.

Immediately, one official waved his arms across his chest, signaling an incomplete pass. It appeared that the game was over, with Washington winning again and gaining a large advantage over their divisional rivals. But there seemed to be a difference of opinion among the officials. Cardinal fans clung to the hope that somehow the officials had spotted something that would give their team another chance.

The officials' debate centered on one point: Had Gray ever had control of the ball, even for a moment? If he had, the play would have to be ruled a touchdown. The fact that he dropped the ball made no difference because it was considered a touchdown the instant he had gained control. The Cardinals, of course, argued that Gray *had* held the ball long enough, while the Redskins claimed that to be ridiculous. They felt Houston had broken up the pass before Gray had ever caught it.

The decision was an important one, not only for that game, but for the entire play-off picture as well. The officials told the teams to back off while they discussed the play. For three minutes, they huddled while the players and the St. Louis fans were nearly driven crazy with suspense.

The meeting finally broke up, and the referee raised both hands over his head. That meant a touchdown for St. Louis. The Cardinals made the extra point and sent the game into overtime.

St. Louis' luck continued as they won the toss to receive the overtime kickoff.

...for world-class sprinter Mel Gray to break away from the defenders.

Jim Bakken put the Redskins out of their misery with this overtime field goal.

With hefty fullback Jim Otis plowing forward behind a talented escort of blockers, the Cardinals advanced 55 yards in 11 plays. That put the ball on the Redskins' 37-yard line, and St. Louis called for their place kicker, Jim Bakken. Bakken calmly kicked the 45-yard field goal to give his team the victory.

The game turned out to be the turning point in the season for both clubs. St. Louis went on to capture their second-straight Eastern Division crown and moved on to the play-offs. The touchdown pass, meanwhile, seemed to pop the Redskins' balloon. They stumbled through their last five games and won only two of them. For the first time in his pro career, Redskin head coach George Allen did not make the play-offs.

The play differed from the Renfro incident of the previous chapter in that several officials stepped forward to make the call. The problem was that they did not immediately agree. Mel

Gray had straddled the line between catching the ball and dropping it. There could hardly have been a closer call for an official to make at such a dramatic time. Perhaps only the fact that the play had to be called one way or the other gave St. Louis the victory and ruined the Redskins' season.

## Touchdown

A Touchdown is the situation in which any part of the ball, legally in possession of a player inbounds, is on, above, or behind the opponents' goal line (plane), provided it is not a touchback.

*Rule 3, Section 40*

## Dead Ball

The ball is automatically dead at the instant of legal player possession on, above, or behind the opponents' goal line.

*Rule 11, Section 2, Article 1*

**Standing tough against the Raider rush, Len Dawson aims for his favorite target and bodyguard, Otis Taylor, early in the game.**

# ★★★**10**★★★

# **Where Were We?**

## *Oakland Raiders vs. Kansas City Chiefs*
### November 1, 1970

Most fans know football's most obvious rules by heart. But there are also a few little-known rules that cover all kinds of whacky circumstances. Woe to the referee who runs into one of those situations! Even though he may be certain about a rule, he's going to have a hard time convincing the team on the short end of the call that he knows what he's doing. This is especially true when the play gets more complicated than a brain teaser. And it doesn't help when the poor official has to sort it all out while thousands of fans are screaming for his hide!

A crew of NFL officials more than earned their pay on a single play during a game in Kansas City on November 1, 1970. Although it was only the halfway point of the season, it was a game that both teams felt they had to win. But both teams—the Kansas City Chiefs and the visiting Oakland Raiders—had been unimpressive so far. Kansas City, the defending Super Bowl champs, had stumbled to a 3 and 3 mark, while Oakland's record stood at 3 wins, 2 losses, and 1 tie. The loser of this game would have little chance of reaching the play-offs at the end of the year, and this pressure made the fierce rivalry between the teams more heated than ever before.

The Chiefs and the Raiders hurled themselves at each other through $3\frac{1}{2}$ quarters with neither team gaining the upper hand. With six minutes to play, Kansas City quarterback Len Dawson threw a touchdown pass to put his team on top, 17 to 14. Then the Chiefs forced the Raiders to punt. If their offense could only put together a few first downs, they could run out the clock and win.

Fred Biletnikoff, who later in the game caught several key Daryle Lamonica passes, came this close to a touchdown against Kansas City cornerback Jim Marsalis.

There were about two minutes left in the contest when the Chiefs faced a difficult third-and-eight situation near midfield. A first down here could just about wrap up the victory, and the Chiefs had a special play for the occasion.

Dawson took the snap from center and stuck the ball in the stomach of a running back. The Raiders were waiting for the ball carrier and stopped him near the line of scrimmage. It was only then that most of them discovered the back didn't have the ball after all! Dawson had cleverly held onto it and was running all alone down the right side of the field. The Raiders had been fooled so thoroughly that the quarterback ran all the way to the Raider 29 and would have gone further had he not tripped over his own teammate. Dawson had made the crucial first down.

Since none of the Raiders had yet touched him, Dawson could have gotten to his feet and kept running for a few extra yards. But before he could do that, Oakland's 280-pound defensive end, Ben Davidson, arrived on the scene. Davidson dove into Dawson's ribs with more enthusiasm than the rules allowed. It was obviously an il-

legal hit, and an official threw a flag on the spot.

The official was not the only one who thought big Ben had played it too rough. Kansas City wide receiver Otis Taylor could not stand seeing his quarterback treated that way and attacked the Raider lineman. Within seconds, the football field was swarming with angry players from both benches.

It took several seconds to cool tempers and to get the field cleared. Once that was accomplished, the officials had to sort out just what had happened. Taylor was kicked out of the game for his attack, and the referee prepared to mark off a 15-yard spearing penalty against Davidson and the Raiders. But the officials mulled over the rules and decided it wasn't *quite* as simple as that. Any player who was kicked out of a game automatically drew an unsportsmanlike conduct penalty. Apparently, that meant that 15 yards had to be walked off against the Chiefs. But because Oakland's Davidson had also drawn a 15-yard penalty and both penalties had occured *after* the play was over, the penalties should have canceled each other out.

A scrambling quarterback is fair game for NFL headhunters, but Chief quarterback Dawson was willing to pay the price. Due to an obscure rule, however, his crucial scramble against the Raiders netted him nothing but sore ribs.

Nearly everyone in the stadium thought that it should have been a Kansas City first down on the Raider 29, but that's not what the officials thought. As the Kansas City fans roared in outrage, the men in the striped shirts started trotting back toward the Chiefs' goal line. They said Dawson had not been tackled before Davidson had run into him, which meant that Davidson's penalty had occured before the whistle and was considered a live-ball foul. Taylor had committed his penalty *after* the play was over, so that one was a dead-ball foul. Citing a little-known rule, the officials declared that when there was a live-ball foul by one team and a dead-ball foul by the other on the same play, the entire down had to be replayed. Dawson's clever fake, long run, and sore ribs had all been for nothing!

The game grew even more confusing for the referee when he tried to find the original line of scrimmage. It turned out that no one remembered exactly where the play had started! The spotters and the chain gang had all assumed that Dawson's first down had counted, so they had moved downfield. Then the near-riot had distracted everyone. The referee finally headed for a telephone and called up the press box, the game statistician, and the television monitor. After getting their opinions, he put the ball near the 50-yard line. At last the teams were ready to play.

Kansas City had no more trick plays. They sent running back Ed Podolak into the line, and he was stopped after gaining only three of the eight yards that he had needed for a first down. The officials were grateful he had not gained eight yards because that would have called for a measurement to see if it had been a first down. And, after all, the referee had only guessed where to put the measuring chains! The Chiefs then punted the ball into the end zone, and the Raiders took over on their 20 with 53 seconds left.

Now Oakland's quarterback, Daryle Lamonica, started rushing his team downfield with a series of short passes, and he completed four of his next five tosses to reach the Kansas City 40. There was only time enough to try a long field goal, and Oakland had one of football's top kickers in George Blanda.

Thanks to the referee's ruling, Oakland's ageless kicker, George Blanda, got a chance to pull yet another game out of the fire.

The 43-year-old veteran was enjoying the finest year of his career, and he saved the game for his team with a 48-yard kick. Kansas City fans were not thrilled with the 17-17 tie, and they were convinced that the officials had lost their minds on a crucial play.

The call turned out to be an important one as the Oakland Raiders beat out the Chiefs for the divisional title by a margin of that one game. According to the rule book, the call had *been* correct. And the entire incident had proved how much trouble a referee can get into—even when he's right!

**Foul and Continuing Action Foul**

If there has been a foul by either team during a down not including: (a) an incompletion, or (b) an illegal recovery of a kick and then a continuing action foul by the opponents after the down ends, Articles 7 & 8 are not in force, and it is a double foul. *Rule 14, Section 1, Article 9*

**Double Foul Without Change of Possession**

If there is a double foul without a change of possession, the penalties are offset and the down is replayed at the previous spot. *Rule 14, Section 3, Article 1*

*The rules appearing at the close of each chapter are from*
Official Rules for Professional Football, *copyright ©*
*by the National Football League, and are used*
*with the permission of the National Football League Properties, Inc.*

**ACKNOWLEDGMENTS:** The photographs are reproduced through the courtesy of: pp. 1, 8, 22, 26, 28, 32, 38, 40, 52, 55, 56, 57, 62, UPI/Bettmann Archive; p. 2, James Biever; pp. 6 (© Vernon J. Biever), 42 (© Dave Cross), 43 (© Manny Rubio), 44 (© Tak Makita), National Football League Properties; p. 10, Dallas Cowboys; pp. 12 (George Gellatly), 13, Detroit Lions; pp. 14, 18, Union-Tribune Publishing Company; pp. 16, 17, 70, Oakland Raiders; pp. 20, 34; 35, 36, 68, Vernon J. Biever; p. 24 (left), Minnesota Vikings; p. 24 (right), Los Angeles Rams; p. 30, Thomas J. Croke; p. 31, New England Patriots (Thomas J. Croke); pp. 46, 49, 51, 64, 66, AP/Wide World Photos; p. 48, Denver Broncos; pp. 60, 61, St. Louis Football Cardinals. Cover photographs by Vernon J. Biever.